HOW TO START A PIZZA SHOP

The Ultimate Guide for Aspiring Pizzapreneurs

Michael Daniel

ALL RIGHTS ARE RESERVED

No part of this publication may be reproduced in any form or by any means, including photocopying, recording, or any other electronic or mechanical methods without the prior written permission of the publisher except in the case of brief quotations embodied in reviews and certain other noncommercial uses permitted by copyrights law.

Copyright © Michael Daniel, 2024.

Table of Contents

Chapter 1 9
The Pizzapreneur's Mindset 9
  1.1 Defining Your Pizza Passion: What Kind of Pizzeria Do You Envision? 9
  1.2 Assessing Your Pizza Prowess: Are You Ready to Be a Pizza Pro? 10
  1.3 Cultivating a Pizza-Positive Mindset: Embracing Challenges & Opportunities 12
  1.4 From Passion to Profit: Turning Your Love of Pizza into a Business 13
  1.5 Identifying Your Ideal Customer: Who's Hungry for Your Pizza? 14
  1.6 Setting SMART Goals: Mapping Your Pizzeria's Path to Success 15
  1.7 Embracing the Pizzapreneur Lifestyle: The Rewards & Responsibilities 16

Chapter 2 20
Crafting Your Pizza Concept 20
  2.1 Defining Your Pizza Identity: What Makes Your Pizzeria Unique? 20
  2.2 Menu Magic: Crafting a Pizza Menu That Sells 21
  2.3 Beyond Pizza: Expanding Your Menu with Sides & Drinks 22
  2.4 Sourcing Superior Ingredients: Choosing Quality Over Cost 23

    2.5 Pricing Your Pizza: Finding the Sweet Spot for Profit & Value 24

    2.6 Design & Ambiance: Creating a Pizzeria Atmosphere That Entices 24

    2.7 Building Your Brand: Telling Your Pizzeria's Story 26

Chapter 3 27

The Business of Pizza 27

    3.1 Choosing the Right Business Structure: Sole Proprietor, Partnership, or LLC? 27

    3.2 Navigating Legal & Regulatory Requirements: Licenses, Permits, & More 28

    3.3 Accounting & Bookkeeping for Pizzeria Success: Tracking Your Dough 29

    3.4 Managing Your Pizzeria Finances: Budgeting, Cash Flow, & Profitability 30

    3.5 Insurance Essentials: Protecting Your Pizzeria from Risk 31

    3.6 Building Your Pizzeria Team: Hiring & Managing Staff 31

    3.7 Establishing Pizzeria Policies & Procedures: Smooth Operations 32

Chapter 4 34

Finding the Perfect Pizzeria Location 34

    4.1 Identifying Your Target Market: Where Are Your Pizza Lovers? 34

    4.2 Location, Location, Location: The Importance of Pizzeria Placement 35

    4.3 Analyzing Demographics & Foot Traffic: Choosing a High-Potential Site.............................. 36

    4.4 Evaluating Lease Agreements: Negotiating the Best Terms for Your Pizzeria 37

    4.5 Designing Your Pizzeria Space: Layout, Functionality, & Flow 38

    4.6 Permitting & Zoning Requirements: Navigating Local Regulations.. 39

    4.7 Construction & Renovation: Bringing Your Pizzeria Vision to Life 39

Chapter 5 41

Equipping Your Pizzeria 41

    5.1 Essential Pizzeria Equipment: Ovens, Prep Tables, & More 41

    5.2 Choosing the Right Pizza Oven: Deck, Conveyor, or Brick? 42

    5.3 Selecting Kitchen Essentials: Mixers, Slicers, & Refrigeration 43

    5.4 Point-of-Sale Systems: Streamlining Transactions & Tracking Sales................................. 44

    5.5 Furniture & Decor: Creating a Welcoming Pizzeria Environment 45

    5.6 Technology Solutions: Online Ordering, Delivery Apps, & More 46

    5.7 Maintenance & Upkeep: Keeping Your Pizzeria Equipment in Top Shape.. 47

Chapter 6 48

Marketing Your Pizzeria 48

6.1 Developing a Marketing Plan: Reaching Your Pizza-Loving Audience 48

6.2 Building Your Pizzeria Brand: Creating a Memorable Identity 49

6.3 Online Marketing: Websites, Social Media, & Email Campaigns 50

6.4 Traditional Marketing: Print Ads, Flyers, & Local Promotions 51

6.5 Public Relations & Community Outreach: Building Pizzeria Buzz 52

6.6 Customer Loyalty Programs: Keeping Your Pizza Fans Coming Back 53

6.7 Tracking & Measuring Results: Analyzing Your Marketing Success 53

Chapter 7 55

Launching Your Pizzeria 55

7.1 Planning Your Grand Opening: Creating a Pizzeria Event to Remember 55

7.2 Building Pre-Opening Buzz: Generating Excitement for Your Pizzeria 56

7.3 Managing Your Soft Opening: Fine-Tuning Operations & Menu 57

7.4 Hosting Your Grand Opening Celebration: Welcoming Your Community 58

7.5 Handling Early Challenges: Learning from Mistakes & Adapting 59

7.6 Establishing Your Pizzeria Reputation: Building Customer Trust 60

7.7 Evaluating Your Launch Success: Setting the Stage for Future Growth 61

Chapter 8 62

Daily Pizzeria Operations 62

8.1 Streamlining Pizzeria Operations: Efficient Systems & Processes 62

8.2 Managing Inventory: Keeping Your Pizzeria Stocked & Organized 63

8.3 Maintaining Food Safety Standards: Ensuring Customer Health 64

8.4 Handling Customer Service: Providing Exceptional Pizza Experiences 65

8.5 Managing Pizzeria Finances: Tracking Sales, Costs, & Profits 66

8.6 Training & Developing Your Team: Creating a High-Performing Staff 67

8.7 Adapting to Seasonal Changes: Catering to Customer Preferences 68

Chapter 9 70

Growing Your Pizzeria Business 70

9.2 Catering & Special Events: Serving Pizza Beyond Your Pizzeria 71

9.3 Franchising Your Pizzeria: Taking Your Brand to New Locations 72

9.4 Offering Delivery & Takeout: Expanding Your Pizzeria's Reach 72

9.5 Exploring Partnerships: Collaborating with Local Businesses 73

9.6 Investing in Technology: Enhancing Efficiency & Customer Experience 74

9.7 Staying Ahead of the Competition: Adapting to Market Trends 75

Chapter 10 77

The Future of Your Pizzeria 77

10.1 Evaluating Your Pizzeria's Success: Measuring Key Performance Indicators 77

10.2 Setting New Goals for Growth: Expanding Your Pizzeria's Reach 78

10.3 Embracing Innovation: New Pizza Trends & Technology 79

10.4 Building a Pizzeria Legacy: Passing on Your Pizza Passion 80

10.6 Giving Back to the Community: Supporting Local Causes 82

10.7 The Pizzapreneur's Journey: Reflecting on Your Pizzeria Success 83

Chapter 1

The Pizzapreneur's Mindset

The journey to opening a successful pizzeria begins with the right mindset. It's about more than just loving pizza; it's about embracing the challenges and opportunities of entrepreneurship, understanding your passion, and having a vision for the kind of pizza experience you want to create. This chapter delves into the essential mindset shifts and self-assessment tools that will set you on the path to becoming a thriving pizzapreneur.

1.1 Defining Your Pizza Passion: What Kind of Pizzeria Do You Envision?

Your passion for pizza is the fuel that will drive your pizzeria forward. Take time to reflect on what truly excites you about pizza and the pizzeria experience.

- **Your Pizzeria Story:** What personal experiences or memories inspire your love for pizza? Maybe it's the joy of sharing a pizza with family and friends, the nostalgia of childhood pizza nights, or the excitement of discovering new flavor combinations.
- **Your Pizza Philosophy:** What values and beliefs do you want your pizzeria to embody? Are you passionate about using locally sourced ingredients, supporting sustainable practices, or creating a welcoming community gathering place?

- **Your Pizzeria Vision:** What kind of atmosphere do you want to create? Is it a casual neighborhood joint, a trendy upscale pizzeria, or a fun family-friendly spot?
- **Your Pizza Style:** What type of pizza do you specialize in? Will you focus on classic Neapolitan pies, creative gourmet pizzas, or a unique fusion style?
- **Your Pizzeria Brand:** What image do you want your pizzeria to project? How will your logo, menu design, and marketing materials reflect your unique personality and pizza philosophy?

By defining your pizza passion, you create a clear vision for your pizzeria and a roadmap for success. This passion will guide your decisions and inspire your team, ultimately leading to a pizzeria that stands out in a crowded market.

1.2 Assessing Your Pizza Prowess: Are You Ready to Be a Pizza Pro?

While passion is essential, a successful pizzeria requires more than just love for pizza. It demands a certain level of pizza prowess and business acumen. This section will help you assess your readiness to become a pizzapreneur:

- **Pizza Knowledge:** How much do you know about pizza-making techniques, ingredients, and equipment? Have you worked in a pizzeria before, or have you honed your skills through personal experimentation?

- **Business Skills:** Do you have experience in business management, marketing, finance, or customer service? If not, are you willing to learn and seek guidance from experts?
- **Entrepreneurial Spirit:** Are you comfortable with risk-taking, decision-making, and problem-solving? Do you have the drive and perseverance to overcome challenges and setbacks?
- **Leadership Abilities:** Can you motivate and inspire a team? Are you capable of managing conflict and building a positive work environment?
- **Financial Resources:** Do you have the necessary funds to start and operate a pizzeria? Have you explored funding options such as loans or investors?
- **Time Commitment:** Are you prepared to dedicate the time and energy required to run a successful pizzeria? This includes long hours, late nights, and weekend work.

Don't be discouraged if you don't have all the answers right now. This assessment is simply a starting point to identify your strengths and weaknesses. You can always acquire new skills and knowledge through training, mentorship, or partnerships. The key is to be honest with yourself and develop a plan to address any gaps in your pizza prowess.

1.3 Cultivating a Pizza-Positive Mindset: Embracing Challenges & Opportunities

The path to pizzeria success is not always smooth. It's a journey filled with challenges, setbacks, and unexpected twists and turns. However, with a pizza-positive mindset, you can turn these obstacles into opportunities for growth and innovation.

- **Embracing Resilience:** View challenges as learning experiences, not failures. Use them as opportunities to adapt, improve, and become a stronger pizzapreneur.
- **Staying Positive:** Maintain a positive attitude, even when things get tough. Your optimism will inspire your team and attract loyal customers.
- **Seeking Solutions:** Don't dwell on problems; focus on finding solutions. Be proactive, resourceful, and creative in overcoming obstacles.
- **Learning from Mistakes:** Everyone makes mistakes. The key is to acknowledge them, learn from them, and move forward. Use your mistakes as stepping stones to success.
- **Celebrating Small Wins:** Don't wait for grand achievements to feel accomplished. Celebrate small victories along the way, as they will fuel your motivation and keep you moving forward.

A pizza-positive mindset is not about ignoring challenges or pretending everything is perfect. It's about approaching difficulties with a constructive attitude, finding creative solutions, and maintaining a hopeful outlook. With this mindset, you'll be better equipped to navigate the ups and downs of pizzeria ownership and emerge as a successful pizzapreneur.

1.4 From Passion to Profit: Turning Your Love of Pizza into a Business

Turning your passion for pizza into a profitable business requires a strategic approach. This section will guide you through the essential steps of transforming your pizza dreams into a thriving pizzeria:

- **Market Research:** Analyze your local market to identify potential customers, competitors, and opportunities. What are the current trends in the pizza industry? What are customers looking for in a pizzeria?
- **Business Plan Development:** Create a comprehensive business plan that outlines your pizzeria's concept, target market, financial projections, marketing strategies, and operational plans.
- **Financial Planning:** Determine your start-up costs, operating expenses, and revenue projections. Secure funding through loans, investors, or personal savings.
- **Menu Development:** Craft a delicious and appealing menu that reflects your pizza philosophy and caters to your target market. Consider offering signature pizzas, seasonal specials, and customizable options.
- **Location Selection:** Choose a strategic location with high visibility, accessibility, and foot traffic. Consider the demographics of the area and the proximity to your target customers.

- **Staffing & Training:** Hire passionate and skilled staff who share your vision for the pizzeria. Provide comprehensive training on pizza-making techniques, customer service, and operational procedures.
- **Marketing & Promotion:** Develop a comprehensive marketing plan to create awareness and attract customers. Utilize online and offline channels, such as social media, local advertising, and community events.
- **Operational Efficiency:** Establish efficient systems and processes for inventory management, food preparation, order fulfillment, and customer service.

By following these steps, you can transform your passion for pizza into a profitable business venture. Remember, starting a pizzeria is a marathon, not a sprint. It requires dedication, hard work, and a willingness to adapt and learn along the way. But with the right mindset and strategies, you can turn your pizza dreams into a reality.

1.5 Identifying Your Ideal Customer: Who's Hungry for Your Pizza?

Understanding your ideal customer is crucial for tailoring your pizzeria's offerings and marketing strategies. Consider the following factors:

- **Demographics:** Age, gender, income level, occupation, education level, and family status. Are you targeting young professionals, families with children, or students?

- **Psychographics:** Interests, values, lifestyle, and personality. Are your customers health-conscious foodies, budget-minded students, or adventurous eaters seeking unique flavor combinations?
- **Behaviors:** Dining habits, spending patterns, and brand loyalty. Do your customers prefer dine-in, takeout, or delivery? How often do they order pizza? Are they loyal to specific brands or open to trying new options?

Once you have a clear picture of your ideal customer, you can tailor your menu, pricing, marketing messages, and overall pizzeria experience to their specific needs and preferences. This targeted approach will help you attract and retain loyal customers who resonate with your brand and keep coming back for more.

1.6 Setting SMART Goals: Mapping Your Pizzeria's Path to Success

Setting SMART goals is essential for achieving success in the pizzeria business. SMART goals are:

- **Specific:** Clearly define what you want to achieve. Instead of saying, "I want to increase sales," specify, "I want to increase sales by 15% in the next quarter."
- **Measurable:** Quantify your goals so you can track your progress. Use metrics such as revenue, profit margin, customer satisfaction ratings, or social media engagement.
- **Achievable:** Set realistic goals that are challenging but attainable. Consider your resources, capabilities, and market conditions.

- **Relevant:** Ensure your goals align with your overall business objectives and pizza passion. Avoid setting goals that are not relevant to your pizzeria's success.
- **Time-Bound:** Establish a timeline for achieving your goals. This will help you stay focused and motivated.

By setting SMART goals, you create a roadmap for your pizzeria's success. You can break down your long-term vision into smaller, actionable steps, track your progress, and make necessary adjustments along the way. This structured approach will help you stay on track and achieve your pizza dreams.

1.7 Embracing the Pizzapreneur Lifestyle: The Rewards & Responsibilities

Being a pizzapreneur is more than just a job; it's a lifestyle. It offers unique rewards and challenges that come with owning and operating your own business.

Rewards:

- **Creative Freedom:** You have the autonomy to create your own pizza concept, menu, and brand identity. You can experiment with new flavors, ingredients, and marketing strategies.
- **Financial Independence:** You have the potential to earn a significant income and build a valuable asset. You can create a legacy for yourself and your family.

Community Impact: You can contribute to your local community by providing jobs, supporting local suppliers, and hosting community events. You can create a space that brings people together and fosters a sense of community.

- **Personal Fulfillment:** You get to pursue your passion for pizza and create something that is uniquely yours. You can express your creativity, build relationships with customers, and make a positive impact on their lives.

Responsibilities:

- **Long Hours and Hard Work:** Running a pizzeria requires a significant time commitment and physical effort. You'll likely be working long hours, including nights and weekends, especially during the initial stages of your business.
- **Financial Risk:** Starting and operating a pizzeria involves financial risk. There's always the possibility that your business may not be profitable, or that unexpected expenses could arise.
- **Stress and Pressure:** Entrepreneurship can be stressful, with the constant pressure to meet deadlines, manage finances, and keep customers happy. You need to be able to handle stress and make difficult decisions under pressure.
- **Employee Management:** Hiring, training, and managing staff can be a challenge. You need to be able to motivate your team, resolve conflicts, and create a positive work environment.

- **Customer Service:** Providing excellent customer service is crucial for the success of your pizzeria. You need to be responsive to customer feedback, address complaints promptly, and go the extra mile to ensure customer satisfaction.

Embracing the Pizzapreneur Lifestyle

The pizzapreneur lifestyle is not for everyone. It requires a unique blend of passion, skills, and resilience. However, for those who are willing to put in the hard work and embrace the challenges, the rewards can be immense.

Before you embark on your pizzeria journey, ask yourself these questions:

- Am I truly passionate about pizza and the pizzeria experience?
- Am I willing to put in the long hours and hard work required to run a successful pizzeria?
- Am I comfortable with financial risk and the pressure of entrepreneurship?
- Do I have the skills and knowledge necessary to manage a business, or am I willing to learn and seek guidance?
- Am I ready to embrace the challenges and opportunities that come with being a pizzapreneur?

If your answers are mostly yes, then you're likely well-suited for the pizzapreneur lifestyle. Remember, it's a journey filled with both ups and downs, but with the right mindset and preparation, you can create a pizzeria that thrives and brings joy to your community.

The Pizzapreneur's Mindset is the foundation upon which a successful pizzeria is built. It's about understanding your passion, assessing your skills, cultivating a positive attitude, setting goals, and embracing the unique lifestyle of a pizzeria owner. By developing the right mindset, you'll be better equipped to navigate the challenges and seize the opportunities that come with turning your love for pizza into a profitable business.

Remember, this is just the first step on your pizzeria journey. As you progress through the following chapters, you'll learn about crafting your pizza concept, developing a business plan, securing funding, finding the perfect location, and much more. But with a solid Pizzapreneur's Mindset, you'll be well-prepared to tackle these challenges and create a pizzeria that is truly your own.

Chapter 2

Crafting Your Pizza Concept

In this chapter, we'll dive into the exciting world of pizza concept development. This is where your pizzeria's unique identity begins to take shape, from the types of pizzas you'll offer to the ambiance of your dining space. A well-crafted pizza concept is the foundation of your brand, attracting customers and setting you apart from the competition.

2.1 Defining Your Pizza Identity: What Makes Your Pizzeria Unique?

Your pizza identity is what distinguishes your pizzeria from all the others. It's a combination of your culinary style, values, and brand personality. To define your pizza identity, consider the following questions:

- **What's your pizza philosophy?** Are you focused on traditional recipes, innovative flavor combinations, or a specific dietary niche (like gluten-free or vegan)?
- **What's your brand personality?** Are you quirky and fun, sophisticated and elegant, or family-friendly and casual?
- **What's your target audience?** Who are you trying to attract with your pizza? Students, families, foodies, or a specific cultural group?
- **What's your unique selling proposition (USP)?** What sets your pizzeria apart from the

competition? Is it your secret sauce, your unique pizza crust, or your commitment to local ingredients?
- **What's your brand story?** What inspired you to open a pizzeria? What are your values and goals?

Once you've answered these questions, you can start to create a brand identity that reflects your unique personality and pizza philosophy. This identity will guide your decisions about your menu, decor, marketing, and overall customer experience.

2.2 Menu Magic: Crafting a Pizza Menu That Sells

Your pizza menu is the heart of your pizzeria. It's where you showcase your culinary creativity and entice customers with delicious offerings. A well-crafted menu should be:

- **Diverse:** Offer a variety of pizzas to appeal to different tastes and dietary preferences. Include classic options as well as unique signature pizzas.
- **Balanced:** Strike a balance between traditional and innovative flavors. Experiment with new toppings and combinations while still offering familiar favorites.
- **Visually Appealing:** Design your menu to be easy to read and visually appealing. Use high-quality photos and descriptions that highlight the unique features of each pizza.
- **Strategically Priced:** Price your pizzas competitively while ensuring profitability.

Consider offering different sizes and pricing tiers to cater to different budgets.
- **Seasonal:** Incorporate seasonal ingredients to keep your menu fresh and exciting. Offer limited-time specials to create a sense of urgency and encourage repeat visits.

Remember, your menu is not just a list of pizzas; it's a reflection of your pizza identity and brand personality. It should tell a story and entice customers to try your delicious creations.

2.3 Beyond Pizza: Expanding Your Menu with Sides & Drinks

While pizza is the star of the show, don't neglect the supporting cast. Sides and drinks can complement your pizza offerings and enhance the overall customer experience. Consider offering:

- **Appetizers:** Garlic knots, breadsticks, salads, wings, or fried appetizers like mozzarella sticks or calamari.
- **Desserts:** Cannoli, tiramisu, gelato, or other Italian-inspired sweets.
- **Beverages:** Soft drinks, iced tea, lemonade, bottled water, beer, wine, or craft cocktails.

When selecting sides and drinks, consider your target audience and pizza concept. Choose items that complement your pizza flavors and enhance the overall dining experience.

2.4 Sourcing Superior Ingredients: Choosing Quality Over Cost

The quality of your ingredients directly impacts the taste and appeal of your pizza. While it's tempting to cut costs by using cheaper ingredients, this can ultimately compromise the quality of your pizza and alienate customers. Invest in high-quality ingredients that are fresh, flavorful, and sourced from reputable suppliers. Consider using:

- **Fresh, locally sourced produce:** Support local farmers and businesses while ensuring the freshest possible ingredients.
- **High-quality cheeses:** Use premium mozzarella, Parmesan, and other cheeses that melt well and add depth of flavor.
- **San Marzano tomatoes:** These Italian tomatoes are known for their sweetness and low acidity, making them ideal for pizza sauce.
- **Specialty meats and toppings:** Offer a variety of high-quality meats, such as pepperoni, sausage, and prosciutto, as well as unique toppings like artisanal mushrooms, roasted vegetables, or imported olives.

By prioritizing quality ingredients, you create a superior pizza that stands out from the competition. Customers will appreciate the difference, and they'll be willing to pay a premium for a pizza made with care and attention to detail.

2.5 Pricing Your Pizza: Finding the Sweet Spot for Profit & Value

Pricing your pizza is a balancing act between profitability and customer perception of value. You need to charge enough to cover your costs and generate a profit, but not so much that you scare away customers. Consider these factors when setting your prices:

- **Cost of ingredients:** Calculate the cost of each ingredient per pizza and factor in any additional costs, such as labor and overhead.
- **Competitor pricing:** Research what other pizzerias in your area are charging for similar pizzas. You don't want to be significantly more expensive than your competitors.
- **Target audience:** Consider the demographics of your target audience and their willingness to pay for pizza.
- **Perceived value:** The quality of your ingredients, the size of your pizzas, and the overall dining experience all contribute to the perceived value of your pizza.

By carefully considering these factors, you can set prices that are both profitable for your business and attractive to your customers.

2.6 Design & Ambiance: Creating a Pizzeria Atmosphere That Entices

The design and ambiance of your pizzeria play a crucial role in attracting and retaining customers. Your space should reflect your brand personality and create a welcoming environment that encourages customers to relax and enjoy their meal. Consider these elements when designing your pizzeria:

- **Layout:** Create a functional layout that maximizes space and ensures smooth traffic flow. Consider separate areas for dining, takeout, and delivery.
- **Lighting:** Use a combination of ambient, task, and accent lighting to create a warm and inviting atmosphere.
- **Colors:** Choose colors that reflect your brand personality and create a cohesive look. Use warm colors to create a cozy feel, or cool colors to create a modern vibe.
- **Furniture:** Select comfortable and durable furniture that complements your pizzeria's style. Consider different seating options, such as booths, tables, and bar stools.
- **Decor:** Add decorative elements that reflect your brand identity and create a unique atmosphere. Use artwork, murals, plants, or other decorative items to personalize your space.
- **Music:** Choose music that complements your pizzeria's atmosphere and enhances the dining experience.

By creating a visually appealing and inviting space, you can attract customers and encourage them to stay longer and order more.

2.7 Building Your Brand: Telling Your Pizzeria's Story

Your brand is more than just a logo and a name; it's the story of your pizzeria and the values it represents. To build a strong brand, you need to tell your story in a way that resonates with your customers.

- **Craft a compelling brand story:** What inspired you to open a pizzeria? What are your values and goals? Share your story through your website, social media, and marketing materials.
- **Develop a consistent brand identity:** Use a consistent logo, color palette, and visual style across all your marketing channels. This will help customers recognize your brand and create a cohesive brand image.
- **Engage with your community:** Participate in local events, sponsor community initiatives, and interact with customers on social media. This will help you build relationships and create a loyal following.
- **Provide excellent customer service:** Go above and beyond to exceed customer expectations. This will create positive word-of-mouth and build a strong reputation for your pizzeria.
- **Live your brand values:** Ensure your actions align with your brand values. This will build trust and credibility with your customers.

By building a strong brand, you create a loyal following of customers who are passionate about your pizzeria. This will lead to repeat business, positive word-of-mouth, and ultimately, long-term success.

Chapter 3

The Business of Pizza

While your passion for pizza fuels your vision, a successful pizzeria requires a solid foundation in business principles. This chapter will guide you through the essential steps of establishing and managing the business side of your pizzeria, from choosing the right legal structure to building a winning team.

3.1 Choosing the Right Business Structure: Sole Proprietor, Partnership, or LLC?

The legal structure you choose for your pizzeria impacts your liability, taxes, and operational flexibility. Here's a brief overview of the most common options:

- **Sole Proprietorship:** The simplest and most common structure for small businesses. You are the sole owner andresponsible for all debts and liabilities.
- **Partnership:** Two or more individuals share ownership and responsibilities. Partnerships can be general (shared liability) or limited (limited liability for some partners).
- **Limited Liability Company (LLC):** Combines the limited liability of a corporation with the tax benefits of a partnership. Offers more flexibility in management and profit distribution.

Consult with a lawyer or accountant to determine the best structure for your specific needs and circumstances. Consider factors such as your risk tolerance, tax implications, and future growth plans.

3.2 Navigating Legal & Regulatory Requirements: Licenses, Permits, & More

Operating a pizzeria involves complying with various legal and regulatory requirements. These may include:

- **Business License:** Required to operate legally in your city or state.
- **Food Service Permit:** Ensures your pizzeria meets health and safety standards.
- **Employer Identification Number (EIN):** Used for tax reporting and employee payroll.
- **Sales Tax Permit:** Allows you to collect and remit sales tax on your products.
- **Liquor License:** If you plan to serve alcohol, you'll need a liquor license.
- **Zoning and Building Permits:** Required for construction or renovation of your pizzeria space.

The specific requirements vary depending on your location. Consult with your local authorities or a lawyer to ensure you obtain all necessary licenses and permits.

3.3 Accounting & Bookkeeping for Pizzeria Success: Tracking Your Dough

Accurate accounting and bookkeeping are essential for managing your pizzeria's finances and making informed business decisions. Key tasks include:

- **Tracking Income and Expenses:** Record all revenue generated and expenses incurred by your pizzeria. This includes sales, cost of goods sold (COGS), labor costs, rent, utilities, and marketing expenses.
- **Financial Statements:** Prepare regular financial statements, such as income statements, balance sheets, and cash flow statements. These statements provide a snapshot of your pizzeria's financial health and performance.
- **Tax Preparation:** Maintain accurate records for tax reporting and compliance. Consult with an accountant to ensure you're meeting all tax obligations.
- **Inventory Management:** Track inventory levels to avoid overstocking or running out of essential ingredients.
- **Payroll:** Manage employee payroll, including calculating wages, withholding taxes, and making timely payments.

Consider using accounting software or hiring a professional bookkeeper to help you manage your pizzeria's finances. Accurate financial records are essential for making informed business decisions, securing funding, and ensuring long-term profitability.

3.4 Managing Your Pizzeria Finances: Budgeting, Cash Flow, & Profitability

Financial management is a critical aspect of running a successful pizzeria. Key areas to focus on include:

- **Budgeting:** Create a comprehensive budget that outlines your projected income and expenses. Review your budget regularly and adjust as needed.
- **Cash Flow Management:** Ensure you have enough cash on hand to cover your expenses and meet your financial obligations. Monitor your cash flow closely and take steps to improve it if necessary.
- **Profitability Analysis:** Analyze your pizzeria's profitability by calculating your gross profit margin, net profit margin, and return on investment (ROI). Identify areas where you can improve your profitability.
- **Pricing Strategy:** Set prices that cover your costs, generate a profit, and remain competitive in the market. Consider offering discounts and promotions strategically to attract customers and boost sales.
- **Cost Control:** Look for ways to reduce expenses without compromising quality. This could involve negotiating better prices with suppliers, reducing waste, or implementing energy-saving measures.

By managing your finances effectively, you can ensure your pizzeria's financial stability and long-term success.

3.5 Insurance Essentials: Protecting Your Pizzeria from Risk

Insurance is crucial for protecting your pizzeria from financial losses due to unexpected events. Key types of insurance to consider include:

- **General Liability Insurance:** Protects your business from claims of bodily injury or property damage caused by your pizzeria or its employees.
- **Property Insurance:** Covers damage to your pizzeria's building and equipment due to fire, theft, vandalism, or natural disasters.
- **Workers' Compensation Insurance:** Provides benefits to employees who are injured or become ill due to their work.
- **Business Interruption Insurance:** Covers lost income and expenses if your pizzeria is forced to close temporarily due to a covered event.
- **Food Contamination Insurance:** Protects your business from liability claims resulting from foodborne illnesses.

Consult with an insurance agent to determine the appropriate coverage for your pizzeria. Having adequate insurance protection can save you from financial ruin in the event of an unforeseen event.

3.6 Building Your Pizzeria Team: Hiring & Managing Staff

Your pizzeria team is essential to your success. They are the face of your brand and responsible for delivering a positive customer experience. When hiring staff, look for individuals who are:

- Passionate about pizza and customer service
- Experienced in food service or willing to learn
- Reliable, responsible, and hardworking
- Team players with a positive attitude

Once you've hired your team, provide comprehensive training on your pizzeria's menu, procedures, and customer service standards. Foster a positive work environment where employees feel valued and motivated.

3.7 Establishing Pizzeria Policies & Procedures: Smooth Operations

Clear policies and procedures ensure smooth operations and consistency in your pizzeria. These guidelines should cover areas such as:

- **Food safety and hygiene:** Establish strict protocols for food handling, preparation, and storage to ensure customer safety and prevent foodborne illnesses.
- **Customer service:** Define standards for customer service, including greeting customers, taking orders, handling complaints, and resolving issues.
- **Employee conduct:** Outline expectations for employee behavior, dress code, attendance, and punctuality.
- **Cash handling:** Implement procedures for handling cash, processing payments, and reconciling daily sales.

- **Inventory management:** Establish procedures for ordering, receiving, storing, and rotating inventory to ensure freshness and prevent waste.
- **Opening and closing procedures:** Create checklists for opening and closing your pizzeria to ensure all tasks are completed and the space is secure.

By establishing clear policies and procedures, you create a structured and efficient work environment where everyone knows their roles and responsibilities. This leads to smoother operations, improved customer service, and ultimately, a more successful pizzeria.

Chapter 4

Finding the Perfect Pizzeria Location

Your pizzeria's location is a critical factor in its success. It can determine your visibility, accessibility, and ultimately, your customer base. This chapter will guide you through the process of finding the perfect spot for your pizzeria, from identifying your target market to navigating local regulations and bringing your vision to life.

4.1 Identifying Your Target Market: Where Are Your Pizza Lovers?

Before you start scouting locations, it's crucial to understand your target market. Who are you trying to attract with your pizza? Are you targeting families, students, young professionals, or a specific cultural group? Once you know who your ideal customers are, you can identify the areas where they live, work, and play. This will help you narrow down your search for the perfect location.

Consider the following factors when identifying your target market:

- **Demographics:** Age, gender, income level, occupation, and family status.
- **Psychographics:** Interests, values, lifestyle, and personality.

- **Behaviors:** Dining habits, spending patterns, and brand preferences.

You can gather this information through market research, surveys, and online analytics. Once you have a clear understanding of your target market, you can start to identify the areas where they are most likely to frequent.

4.2 Location, Location, Location: The Importance of Pizzeria Placement

The old adage "location, location, location" is especially true for pizzerias. A good location can make or break your business. Here's why:

- **Visibility:** A highly visible location will attract more foot traffic and drive-by customers.
- **Accessibility:** Choose a location that's easy for customers to reach by car, public transportation, or foot. Ample parking is also essential.
- **Competition:** Consider the level of competition in the area. While some competition is healthy, too much can make it difficult to stand out.
- **Foot Traffic:** Look for areas with high foot traffic, especially during your target hours of operation.
- **Rent/Lease Costs:** Factor in the cost of rent or lease when evaluating potential locations. You don't want to overextend your budget.

- **Zoning and Regulations:** Ensure the location is zoned for commercial use and complies with local regulations.

Finding the right balance of these factors can be challenging, but it's essential for your pizzeria's success. Take your time, do your research, and don't settle for a less-than-ideal location.

4.3 Analyzing Demographics & Foot Traffic: Choosing a High-Potential Site

Once you've identified potential locations, it's time to analyze the demographics and foot traffic of each area. This will help you determine which locations have the highest potential for your pizzeria.

- **Demographics:** Look at the age, income level, and lifestyle of the residents in the area. Does the area match your target market?
- **Foot Traffic:** Observe the foot traffic during different times of day and week. Are there enough potential customers passing by?
- **Competition:** Assess the competition in the area. How many other pizzerias are there? What are their strengths and weaknesses?
- **Accessibility and Parking:** Is the location easily accessible by car and public transportation? Is there ample parking available?
- **Visibility:** How visible is the location from the street? Is there signage potential?

By analyzing these factors, you can choose a location that's most likely to attract and retain customers.

4.4 Evaluating Lease Agreements: Negotiating the Best Terms for Your Pizzeria

Once you've found a potential location, it's time to negotiate the lease agreement. This is a crucial step, as the terms of your lease can significantly impact your pizzeria's profitability. Key terms to negotiate include:

- **Rent:** Negotiate the monthly rent, as well as any potential rent increases over the term of the lease.
- **Term:** Determine the length of the lease. A longer lease provides more stability, but a shorter lease offers more flexibility.
- **Security Deposit:** Negotiate the amount of the security deposit required.
- **Maintenance and Repairs:** Clarify who is responsible for maintenance and repairs.
- **Subletting:** Determine if subletting is allowed, in case you need to relocate or close your business.
- **Renewal Options:** Negotiate options for renewing the lease at the end of the term.

Consult with a lawyer or commercial real estate agent to help you understand the lease agreement and negotiate favorable terms.

4.5 Designing Your Pizzeria Space: Layout, Functionality, & Flow

The layout of your pizzeria should be functional, efficient, and inviting. Consider these factors when designing your space:

- **Customer Flow:** Create a clear path for customers to enter, order, and dine. Avoid bottlenecks and ensure there's enough space for customers to move around comfortably.
- **Kitchen Design:** Design a kitchen that's efficient and conducive to food preparation. Consider the placement of ovens, prep stations, storage, and dishwashing areas.
- **Dining Area:** Create a comfortable and inviting dining area that reflects your brand personality. Choose furniture that's both stylish and durable.
- **Takeout and Delivery:** If you offer takeout or delivery, design a designated area for these services. This will help streamline operations and prevent congestion.
- **Restrooms:** Ensure your restrooms are clean, accessible, and well-maintained.

A well-designed pizzeria space can enhance the customer experience and improve operational efficiency.

4.6 Permitting & Zoning Requirements: Navigating Local Regulations

Before you can open your pizzeria, you'll need to obtain the necessary permits and comply with local zoning regulations. These requirements vary depending on your location, but typically include:

- **Zoning Permit:** Ensures your pizzeria is located in an area zoned for commercial use.
- **Building Permit:** Required for any construction or renovation of your pizzeria space.
- **Health Permit:** Ensures your pizzeria meets health and safety standards for food preparation and service.
- **Fire Safety Permit:** Ensures your pizzeria has adequate fire safety measures in place.
- **Sign Permit:** If you plan to install signage, you may need a sign permit.

Consult with your local authorities to determine the specific permitting and zoning requirements for your area.

4.7 Construction & Renovation: Bringing Your Pizzeria Vision to Life

Once you've secured the necessary permits, you can begin construction or renovation of your pizzeria space. This is where your vision starts to become a reality. Work with a qualified contractor to ensure the project is completed on time and within budget.

During the construction process, stay involved and ensure that the work is being done according to your specifications. Regularly inspect the progress and communicate with your contractor to address any issues that may arise.

Once construction is complete, it's time to furnish and decorate your pizzeria. Choose furniture, lighting, and decor that reflect your brand identity and create a welcoming atmosphere for your customers.

Finding the perfect pizzeria location is a multi-faceted process that requires careful planning and research. By identifying your target market, analyzing demographics and foot traffic, evaluating lease agreements, designing a functional space, and navigating local regulations, you can find a location that sets your pizzeria up for success. Remember, the perfect location is not just about finding a space that meets your needs; it's about finding a space that resonates with your brand and attracts your ideal customers.

Chapter 5

Equipping Your Pizzeria

In this chapter, we'll delve into the essential equipment and technology that will transform your pizzeria vision into a functional and efficient reality. From the heart of your operation – the pizza oven – to the point-of-sale system that streamlines transactions, each piece of equipment plays a vital role in the success of your pizzeria.

5.1 Essential Pizzeria Equipment: Ovens, Prep Tables, & More

Equipping your pizzeria is a significant investment, but it's crucial for ensuring smooth operations and delivering high-quality pizzas. Here's a list of essential equipment you'll need:

- **Pizza Oven:** The heart of your pizzeria. Choose a model that suits your pizza style, production volume, and budget.
- **Prep Tables:** Stainless steel tables for preparing dough, toppings, and assembling pizzas.
- **Refrigeration:** Reach-in refrigerators and freezers for storing ingredients, dough, and prepped toppings.
- **Dough Mixer:** A commercial mixer for efficiently mixing large batches of dough.
- **Dough Sheeter:** A machine for rolling out dough evenly and consistently.

- **Pizza Peel:** A wooden or metal paddle for transferring pizzas in and out of the oven.
- **Pizza Cutter:** A sharp cutter for slicing pizzas quickly and evenly.
- **Serving Utensils:** Plates, napkins, cups, and other utensils for serving customers.
- **Ventilation System:** A powerful ventilation system to remove smoke, heat, and odors from the kitchen.
- **Dishwashing Equipment:** A commercial dishwasher for efficient cleaning and sanitization.

This is just a starting point. Depending on your menu and service style, you may need additional equipment, such as a deep fryer for appetizers, a gelato machine for desserts, or a delivery vehicle for catering orders.

5.2 Choosing the Right Pizza Oven: Deck, Conveyor, or Brick?

Your pizza oven is the most important piece of equipment in your pizzeria. It directly affects the quality and consistency of your pizzas. The three main types of pizza ovens are:

- **Deck Ovens:** Traditional ovens with stone or brick decks that bake pizzas directly on the surface. They produce pizzas with a crispy crust and even bake.
- **Conveyor Ovens:** High-volume ovens that move pizzas through a conveyor belt. They are efficient for cooking large quantities of pizza quickly.

- **Brick Ovens:** Wood-fired or gas-fired ovens that create a unique flavor profile. They are ideal for Neapolitan-style pizzas but require skilled operators.

Consider your pizza style, production volume, and budget when choosing a pizza oven. If you're focusing on Neapolitan-style pizzas, a brick oven is a must. If you need to cook large quantities of pizza quickly, a conveyor oven may be a better option.

5.3 Selecting Kitchen Essentials: Mixers, Slicers, & Refrigeration

In addition to the pizza oven, there are other essential kitchen equipment pieces you'll need:

- **Commercial Mixer:** A powerful mixer for efficiently mixing large batches of dough. Look for a mixer with a spiral dough hook for optimal gluten development.
- **Vegetable Slicer:** A slicer for quickly and evenly slicing vegetables for toppings.
- **Meat Slicer:** A slicer for thinly slicing meats like pepperoni and prosciutto.
- **Refrigeration:** Adequate refrigeration is essential for storing ingredients, dough, and prepped toppings. Choose commercial-grade refrigerators and freezers that can handle the demands of a busy pizzeria.

Invest in high-quality kitchen equipment that is durable, reliable, and easy to clean. This will ensure your pizzeria runs smoothly and produces consistently delicious pizzas.

5.4 Point-of-Sale Systems: Streamlining Transactions & Tracking Sales

A point-of-sale (POS) system is a computerized system for processing transactions, tracking sales, and managing inventory. A good POS system can streamline your pizzeria's operations and provide valuable insights into your business. Key features to look for in a POS system include:

- **Order Management:** Ability to take orders, track orders in progress, and manage delivery and takeout orders.
- **Payment Processing:** Accept various payment methods, including cash, credit cards, and mobile payments.
- **Inventory Management:** Track inventory levels, generate purchase orders, and alert you when items are running low.
- **Sales Reporting:** Generate detailed reports on sales, customer behavior, and inventory usage.
- **Employee Management:** Track employee hours, manage schedules, and calculate payroll.
- **Customer Relationship Management (CRM):** Store customer information, track purchase history, and send targeted marketing messages.

Choosing the right POS system can significantly improve your pizzeria's efficiency and profitability. Research different options and choose a system that meets your specific needs and budget.

5.5 Furniture & Decor: Creating a Welcoming Pizzeria Environment

The ambiance of your pizzeria plays a crucial role in attracting and retaining customers. Your furniture and decor should reflect your brand personality and create a welcoming environment that encourages customers to relax and enjoy their meal. Consider these factors when choosing furniture and decor:

- **Style:** Choose furniture and decor that complement your pizzeria's concept and target audience. A family-friendly pizzeria might opt for casual and colorful furniture, while an upscale pizzeria might choose more elegant and sophisticated pieces.
- **Comfort:** Your customers should feel comfortable and relaxed while dining. Choose chairs and booths with ample padding and support.
- **Durability:** Pizzeria furniture needs to withstand heavy use. Choose materials that are durable and easy to clean.
- **Functionality:** Your furniture should be functional as well as stylish. Consider tables that are easy to move and chairs that can be stacked for storage.

Don't forget about the details. Artwork, plants, lighting, and music can all contribute to the overall ambiance of your pizzeria.

5.6 Technology Solutions: Online Ordering, Delivery Apps, & More

Technology plays an increasingly important role in the restaurant industry. By embracing technology solutions, you can streamline operations, improve customer service, and reach a wider audience. Consider these technology options for your pizzeria:

- **Online Ordering:** Allow customers to place orders online through your website or a third-party platform. This can increase convenience for customers and reduce the workload for your staff.
- **Delivery Apps:** Partner with popular delivery apps like Uber Eats or DoorDash to expand your delivery reach and attract new customers.
- **Tabletop Ordering Tablets:** Allow customers to browse the menu, place orders, and pay their bill at their table. This can improve order accuracy and efficiency.
- **Customer Loyalty Programs:** Implement a digital loyalty program to reward repeat customers and encourage loyalty.
- **Social Media Marketing:** Use social media platforms to engage with customers, promote your pizzeria, and build brand awareness.

By embracing technology, you can stay ahead of the curve and provide your customers with the best possible experience.

5.7 Maintenance & Upkeep: Keeping Your Pizzeria Equipment in Top Shape

Proper maintenance and upkeep of your pizzeria equipment are essential for ensuring longevity, efficiency, and safety. Create a maintenance schedule for each piece of equipment and follow the manufacturer's recommendations for cleaning and servicing.

Regularly inspect your equipment for signs of wear and tear, and address any issues promptly. This will prevent costly breakdowns and ensure your pizzeria runs smoothly. Consider establishing relationships with local service providers who can provide timely repairs and maintenance services.

By investing in quality equipment and maintaining it properly, you can ensure that your pizzeria operates efficiently and produces consistently delicious pizzas for years to come.

Chapter 6

Marketing Your Pizzeria

Your pizzeria's marketing strategy is the key to attracting and retaining customers. In this chapter, we'll explore various marketing techniques, both online and offline, to help you reach your target audience, build brand awareness, and create a loyal following of pizza enthusiasts.

6.1 Developing a Marketing Plan: Reaching Your Pizza-Loving Audience

A comprehensive marketing plan outlines your pizzeria's goals, target audience, strategies, and tactics. It serves as a roadmap for your marketing efforts, ensuring that your messages resonate with your ideal customers and drive results. Your marketing plan should include:

- **Marketing Goals:** What do you want to achieve with your marketing efforts? Increase brand awareness, drive traffic to your pizzeria, or boost online orders?
- **Target Audience:** Who are you trying to reach with your marketing messages? Define your ideal customers based on demographics, psychographics, and behaviors.
- **Marketing Channels:** Which channels will you use to reach your target audience? Consider online channels like social media, email marketing, and search engine optimization

(SEO), as well as offline channels like print advertising, direct mail, and community events.
- **Marketing Budget:** How much are you willing to spend on marketing? Allocate your budget across different channels based on their effectiveness and your target audience.
- **Marketing Calendar:** Create a timeline for your marketing activities, outlining when and how you'll execute each strategy.
- **Evaluation and Measurement:** Track the results of your marketing campaigns and analyze their effectiveness. This will help you identify what's working and what needs improvement.

By developing a well-defined marketing plan, you can ensure that your marketing efforts are targeted, effective, and aligned with your pizzeria's goals.

6.2 Building Your Pizzeria Brand: Creating a Memorable Identity

Your pizzeria's brand is more than just a logo and a name; it's the emotional connection you create with your customers. A strong brand identity sets you apart from the competition and fosters loyalty among your customers. To build a memorable brand, consider the following:

- **Brand Story:** Develop a compelling brand story that resonates with your target audience. Share your passion for pizza, your unique recipes, and your commitment to quality ingredients.

- **Visual Identity:** Create a visually appealing logo, color palette, and font that reflect your brand personality. Use these elements consistently across all your marketing materials.
- **Brand Voice:** Develop a consistent brand voice that speaks to your target audience. Use language that's engaging, authentic, and aligned with your brand personality.
- **Brand Experience:** Ensure that your brand identity is reflected in every aspect of your pizzeria, from the decor and ambiance to the customer service and menu.

A strong brand identity helps customers connect with your pizzeria on a deeper level, making them more likely to choose your pizza over the competition.

6.3 Online Marketing: Websites, Social Media, & Email Campaigns

In today's digital age, online marketing is essential for reaching your target audience. Here are some key online marketing strategies for your pizzeria:

- **Website:** Create a user-friendly website that showcases your menu, location, hours, and contact information. Optimize your website for search engines to improve your online visibility.
- **Social Media:** Use social media platforms like Facebook, Instagram, and Twitter to engage with customers, share photos of your delicious pizzas, and promote special offers.
- **Email Marketing:** Build an email list and send out regular newsletters with promotions,

updates, and behind-the-scenes glimpses of your pizzeria.
- **Online Advertising:** Consider running targeted ads on social media or search engines to reach a wider audience.
- **Online Reviews:** Encourage customers to leave reviews on platforms like Google My Business and Yelp. Positive reviews can boost your online reputation and attract new customers.

By leveraging online marketing channels, you can reach a wider audience, build brand awareness, and drive traffic to your pizzeria.

6.4 Traditional Marketing: Print Ads, Flyers, & Local Promotions

While online marketing is important, don't neglect traditional marketing tactics. They can still be effective in reaching certain segments of your target audience. Consider these options:

- **Print Advertising:** Place ads in local newspapers, magazines, or community newsletters.
- **Flyers and Brochures:** Distribute flyers and brochures in your neighborhood or at local events.
- **Direct Mail:** Send out postcards or coupons to targeted households in your area.
- **Local Partnerships:** Partner with other local businesses to cross-promote each other's products or services.

- **Community Events:** Participate in local events or festivals to showcase your pizza and connect with potential customers.

By combining online and offline marketing strategies, you can reach a wider audience and create a multi-faceted marketing campaign that drives results.

6.5 Public Relations & Community Outreach: Building Pizzeria Buzz

Public relations (PR) and community outreach can help you build buzz around your pizzeria and establish yourself as a valued member of the community. Consider these tactics:

- **Press Releases:** Send out press releases to local media outlets to announce your grand opening, new menu items, or special events.
- **Media Relations:** Build relationships with local journalists and food bloggers. Invite them to your pizzeria for a tasting or offer them exclusive interviews.
- **Community Partnerships:** Partner with local charities or organizations to host fundraising events or donate a portion of your sales to a worthy cause.
- **Social Media Contests:** Run contests or giveaways on social media to engage your audience and generate excitement.

By actively engaging with your community, you can build goodwill, foster loyalty, and create positive word-of-mouth for your pizzeria.

6.6 Customer Loyalty Programs: Keeping Your Pizza Fans Coming Back

A customer loyalty program is a great way to reward your regular customers and incentivize them to keep coming back. Consider these options:

- **Punch Cards:** Offer a free pizza after a certain number of purchases.
- **Points-Based System:** Award points for each purchase, which can be redeemed for discounts or free items.
- **VIP Programs:** Offer exclusive perks, such as early access to new menu items or special discounts, to your most loyal customers.
- **Birthday Rewards:** Send out birthday coupons or free pizzas to customers on their special day.

By rewarding your loyal customers, you can foster a sense of community and encourage repeat business.

6.7 Tracking & Measuring Results: Analyzing Your Marketing Success

To ensure your marketing efforts are effective, it's crucial to track and measure your results. This involves collecting data on various metrics, such as:

- **Website Traffic:** Track the number of visitors to your website, where they're coming from, and which pages they're visiting.

- **Social Media Engagement:** Monitor your social media followers, likes, shares, and comments.
- **Email Open and Click-Through Rates:** Track how many people open your emails and click on the links within them.
- **Sales Data:** Analyze your sales data to see which marketing campaigns are driving the most revenue.
- **Customer Feedback:** Collect feedback from customers through surveys, online reviews, and social media.

By analyzing this data, you can identify which marketing channels are most effective, which messages resonate with your audience, and which areas need improvement. This will help you refine your marketing strategy and achieve greater success.

Marketing is an ongoing process that requires constant attention and adaptation. By developing a comprehensive marketing plan, building a strong brand identity, leveraging online and offline channels, engaging with your community, and tracking your results, you can create a marketing strategy that drives traffic to your pizzeria, builds a loyal following, and ultimately, leads to long-term success. Remember, marketing is not just about selling pizzas; it's about building relationships with your customers and creating a brand that they love and trust.

Chapter 7

Launching Your Pizzeria

The culmination of your hard work and planning is finally here: the grand opening of your pizzeria! This chapter will guide you through the exciting process of launching your business, from building pre-opening buzz to handling early challenges and establishing a stellar reputation.

7.1 Planning Your Grand Opening: Creating a Pizzeria Event to Remember

Your grand opening is your chance to make a big splash and introduce your pizzeria to the community. It should be a memorable event that generates excitement and leaves a lasting impression on your customers. Here's how to plan a grand opening that's truly unforgettable:

- **Set a Date:** Choose a date that works for your schedule and allows enough time for pre-opening preparations. Consider factors like holidays, local events, and weather conditions.
- **Create a Theme:** Develop a theme that aligns with your pizzeria's brand and target audience. This could be a pizza-themed party, a live music event, or a family-friendly celebration.
- **Offer Promotions:** Entice customers with special offers, discounts, or giveaways. Consider offering a free slice of pizza to the first 100

customers or a discount on all pizzas for the first week.
- **Invite Guests:** Invite local media, influencers, community leaders, and potential customers to your grand opening. This will help spread the word and generate buzz.
- **Entertainment:** Provide entertainment to keep guests engaged. This could be a live band, a DJ, face painting for kids, or even a pizza-tossing demonstration.
- **Decorations:** Decorate your pizzeria to reflect the grand opening theme. Use balloons, banners, and signage to create a festive atmosphere.
- **Food and Drinks:** Ensure you have enough food and drinks to cater to your expected number of guests. Consider offering samples of your menu items or signature cocktails.
- **Staffing:** Make sure you have enough staff on hand to handle the crowd and provide excellent customer service.

By carefully planning your grand opening, you can create a memorable event that sets the stage for your pizzeria's success.

7.2 Building Pre-Opening Buzz: Generating Excitement for Your Pizzeria

Before your grand opening, it's essential to build anticipation and excitement among your target audience. This will help ensure a successful launch and generate initial interest in your pizzeria. Here are some strategies for building pre-opening buzz:

- **Social Media:** Use social media platforms to announce your upcoming opening, share behind-the-scenes glimpses of your pizzeria, and offer exclusive sneak peeks of your menu.
- **Email Marketing:** If you have an email list, send out teasers and updates about your progress towards opening. Offer exclusive discounts or promotions to email subscribers.
- **Local Media:** Reach out to local newspapers, radio stations, and online publications to let them know about your pizzeria. Offer them exclusive interviews or stories to generate media coverage.
- **Partnerships:** Partner with local businesses to cross-promote each other. This could involve offering discounts to each other's customers or hosting joint events.
- **Community Outreach:** Get involved in your local community by sponsoring events, donating to charities, or participating in local festivals. This will help build goodwill and create a positive image for your pizzeria.

By generating pre-opening buzz, you can create a sense of anticipation and excitement that will translate into a successful grand opening and a loyal customer base.

7.3 Managing Your Soft Opening: Fine-Tuning Operations & Menu

Before you officially open your doors, consider hosting a soft opening. This is a trial run where you invite a limited number of guests to test your menu, service, and operations. A soft opening allows you to:

- **Fine-tune your menu:** Get feedback on your pizza recipes and make adjustments based on customer preferences.
- **Test your service:** Identify any bottlenecks or inefficiencies in your service flow and make necessary improvements.
- **Train your staff:** Ensure your staff is comfortable with the menu, ordering process, and customer service standards.
- **Get feedback:** Gather valuable feedback from customers on their overall experience. This will help you identify areas for improvement before your grand opening.

A successful soft opening can help you iron out any kinks in your operations and ensure that your grand opening goes smoothly.

7.4 Hosting Your Grand Opening Celebration: Welcoming Your Community

Your grand opening is your chance to welcome your community to your pizzeria and showcase everything you have to offer. It's a celebration of your hard work and dedication, and it should be a fun and festive event for everyone.

- **Follow Your Plan:** Execute the grand opening plan you created earlier. Make sure everything is in place, from decorations and entertainment to staffing and food.
- **Greet Guests:** Personally welcome guests and thank them for coming. Make them feel special and appreciated.

- **Offer Promotions:** Give away free samples, offer discounts, or run contests to entice customers to try your pizza and return for more.
- **Collect Feedback:** Encourage customers to share their feedback on your menu, service, and overall experience. This will help you improve and grow your business.

Your grand opening is not just about making sales; it's about building relationships with your community and establishing your pizzeria as a go-to destination for delicious pizza.

7.5 Handling Early Challenges: Learning from Mistakes & Adapting

No launch is perfect. You're likely to encounter some challenges in the early days of your pizzeria. It's important to remain calm, learn from your mistakes, and adapt your strategies as needed. Some common challenges you may face include:

- **Staffing Issues:** You may have trouble finding qualified staff or experience high turnover rates.
- **Operational Glitches:** You may encounter unexpected problems with your equipment, inventory, or ordering system.
- **Customer Complaints:** You may receive negative feedback from customers about your food, service, or atmosphere.

Don't be discouraged by these challenges. Instead, view them as opportunities for growth and improvement. Listen to feedback, address issues promptly, and make necessary changes to ensure your pizzeria runs smoothly and meets customer expectations.

7.6 Establishing Your Pizzeria Reputation: Building Customer Trust

Your pizzeria's reputation is built on trust. Customers need to trust that your food is delicious, your service is excellent, and your pizzeria is a clean and safe environment. To establish a strong reputation, focus on:

- **Quality Ingredients:** Use fresh, high-quality ingredients to create delicious pizzas that customers will crave.
- **Consistency:** Ensure that your pizzas are consistently delicious every time. This means training your staff properly and adhering to strict quality control standards.
- **Cleanliness:** Maintain a clean and sanitary environment in your kitchen and dining area.
- **Customer Service:** Provide friendly and attentive service that makes customers feel valued and appreciated.
- **Online Presence:** Respond to online reviews and engage with customers on social media. This shows that you care about their feedback and are committed to providing a positive experience.

By focusing on these factors, you can build a reputation for excellence that will attract and retain loyal customers.

7.7 Evaluating Your Launch Success: Setting the Stage for Future Growth

After your grand opening, take some time to evaluate your launch success. Analyze your sales data, customer feedback, and operational efficiency. Identify areas where you exceeded expectations and areas that need improvement. Use this information to refine your strategies and set the stage for future growth.

Consider these questions when evaluating your launch:

- Did you meet your sales goals?
- Did you receive positive feedback from customers?
- Were there any operational issues that need to be addressed?
- Did your marketing campaigns generate the desired results?
- What can you do to improve your pizzeria's performance in the future?

By analyzing your launch success, you can learn valuable lessons and make informed decisions that will help your pizzeria thrive in the long run

Chapter 8

Daily Pizzeria Operations

Welcome to the heart of your pizzeria's day-to-day activities! This chapter focuses on the essential operational aspects that keep your business running smoothly, ensuring customer satisfaction, maintaining food safety, and maximizing profitability.

8.1 Streamlining Pizzeria Operations: Efficient Systems & Processes

Efficiency is key to a successful pizzeria. Streamlined operations ensure orders are fulfilled promptly, customers are satisfied, and your team works cohesively. Here's how to optimize your processes:

- **Standardized Recipes:** Create clear and concise recipes for all menu items, ensuring consistency in taste and quality.
- **Inventory Management System:** Implement a system for tracking inventory levels, ordering supplies, and minimizing waste.
- **Order Management System:** Utilize a POS system or online ordering platform to manage orders efficiently, track delivery times, and process payments seamlessly.
- **Staff Scheduling:** Create optimal staff schedules to ensure adequate coverage during peak hours and minimize labor costs.
- **Communication Channels:** Establish clear communication channels between kitchen staff,

front-of-house staff, and management to ensure smooth coordination.
- **Regular Cleaning and Maintenance:** Maintain a clean and organized workspace to promote efficiency and hygiene.
- **Technology Integration:** Embrace technology solutions like kitchen display systems (KDS) and online ordering platforms to streamline operations.

By implementing efficient systems and processes, you can reduce errors, minimize waste, and maximize productivity.

8.2 Managing Inventory: Keeping Your Pizzeria Stocked & Organized

Effective inventory management is crucial for ensuring you have enough supplies to meet customer demand without overspending or wasting ingredients.

- **Inventory Tracking:** Keep track of your inventory levels using a spreadsheet or inventory management software. This will help you identify trends in ingredient usage and forecast future needs.
- **Par Levels:** Set par levels for each ingredient, indicating the minimum amount you need to have on hand at all times. This will help you avoid running out of essential items.
- **Regular Stocktaking:** Conduct regular inventory checks to ensure accuracy and identify any discrepancies.

- **FIFO (First In, First Out):** Rotate your inventory so that older items are used first, ensuring freshness and preventing waste.
- **Supplier Relationships:** Build strong relationships with your suppliers to ensure timely deliveries and negotiate favorable prices.

Proper inventory management will help you control costs, reduce waste, and ensure you always have the necessary ingredients to serve your customers.

8.3 Maintaining Food Safety Standards: Ensuring Customer Health

Food safety is a top priority for any food service establishment. Adhering to strict food safety standards protects your customers' health and safeguards your pizzeria's reputation. Key practices include:

- **Personal Hygiene:** Ensure all staff members wash their hands thoroughly and frequently, wear gloves when handling food, and avoid touching their face or hair.
- **Proper Food Handling:** Follow safe food handling practices, such as cooking food to proper temperatures, storing food at safe temperatures, and preventing cross-contamination.
- **Cleanliness and Sanitation:** Maintain a clean and sanitary environment in your kitchen and dining area. Sanitize surfaces regularly, clean equipment after each use, and dispose of waste properly.

- **Temperature Control:** Monitor food temperatures regularly to ensure they are within safe zones. Use thermometers to check the internal temperature of cooked food.
- **Allergen Awareness:** Be aware of common food allergens and take steps to prevent cross-contamination. Clearly label menu items that contain allergens.
- **Staff Training:** Provide comprehensive food safety training to all employees and ensure they understand and follow all safety protocols.

By prioritizing food safety, you demonstrate your commitment to customer well-being and build trust in your brand.

8.4 Handling Customer Service: Providing Exceptional Pizza Experiences

Excellent customer service is essential for creating a loyal customer base and positive word-of-mouth. Train your staff to:

- Greet customers warmly and promptly.
- Take orders accurately and efficiently.
- Address any questions or concerns politely and professionally.
- Deliver food promptly and with a smile.
- Check in with customers to ensure their satisfaction.
- Resolve any complaints or issues quickly and effectively.

Encourage your staff to go above and beyond to exceed customer expectations. This could involve offering complimentary breadsticks, remembering regular customers' orders, or accommodating special requests.

Remember, your customers are the lifeblood of your business. By providing exceptional service, you create a positive experience that encourages repeat visits and loyalty.

8.5 Managing Pizzeria Finances: Tracking Sales, Costs, & Profits

Keeping a close eye on your finances is essential for the long-term success of your pizzeria. This involves:

- **Daily Sales Reconciliation:** Reconcile daily sales to ensure accuracy and identify any discrepancies.
- **Cost Tracking:** Track all expenses, including food costs, labor costs, rent, utilities, and marketing expenses.
- **Profitability Analysis:** Calculate your gross profit margin, net profit margin, and return on investment (ROI) regularly. This will help you identify areas where you can improve profitability.
- **Financial Forecasting:** Use your sales and expense data to forecast future financial performance. This will help you plan for growth and make informed business decisions.
- **Budgeting:** Create a realistic budget and stick to it. This will help you manage your cash flow and avoid overspending.

By staying on top of your finances, you can make informed decisions that will ensure your pizzeria's profitability and long-term success.

8.6 Training & Developing Your Team: Creating a High-Performing Staff

Your staff is your pizzeria's most valuable asset. Invest in their training and development to create a high-performing team that is motivated, skilled, and committed to your pizzeria's success.

- **Onboarding and Orientation:** Provide new employees with a thorough onboarding process that covers your pizzeria's mission, values, policies, and procedures.
- **Skills Training:** Offer ongoing training on pizza-making techniques, customer service, food safety, and other relevant skills.
- **Leadership Development:** Identify and develop potential leaders within your team. Provide them with opportunities to grow and take on more responsibility.
- **Performance Reviews:** Conduct regular performance reviews to provide feedback, recognize achievements, and identify areas for improvement.
- **Incentives and Rewards:** Offer incentives and rewards for outstanding performance to motivate your team and boost morale.

By investing in your team, you create a positive work environment, reduce turnover, and improve overall performance.

8.7 Adapting to Seasonal Changes: Catering to Customer Preferences

Customer preferences and demands can change throughout the year. To stay ahead of the curve, it's essential to adapt your menu and marketing strategies to seasonal changes.

- **Seasonal Ingredients:** Incorporate seasonal ingredients into your menu to keep it fresh and exciting.
- **Limited-Time Offers:** Offer seasonal specials or limited-time pizzas to create a sense of urgency and encourage repeat visits.
- **Holiday Promotions:** Run special promotions during holidays or major events to attract customers and boost sales.
- **Weather-Dependent Offerings:** Adjust your menu to accommodate weather conditions. Offer heartier pizzas during colder months and lighter options during warmer months.

By adapting to seasonal changes, you can keep your pizzeria relevant and appeal to a wider range of customers throughout the year.

The day-to-day operations of your pizzeria are the backbone of your business. By streamlining processes, managing inventory, maintaining food safety standards, providing exceptional customer service, managing finances, training your team, and adapting to seasonal changes, you can ensure that your pizzeria runs smoothly, delivers a positive customer experience, and achieves long-term success. Remember, your pizzeria is more than just a place to get pizza; it's a community hub, a place where memories are made, and a reflection of your passion and dedication.

Chapter 9

Growing Your Pizzeria Business

Congratulations! You've successfully launched your pizzeria and established a solid foundation. Now it's time to focus on growth. This chapter explores various strategies for expanding your pizzeria business, from introducing new menu items to embracing technology and adapting to market trends.

9.1 Expanding Your Menu: Introducing New Pizzas & Offerings

Expanding your menu is a great way to keep your customers engaged and attract new ones. Consider the following:

- **New Pizza Flavors:** Experiment with new flavor combinations and unique toppings to create signature pizzas that set you apart.
- **Seasonal Specials:** Offer limited-time pizzas featuring seasonal ingredients to keep your menu fresh and exciting.
- **Non-Pizza Items:** Expand your menu beyond pizza with appetizers, salads, sandwiches, desserts, or even a breakfast pizza.
- **Catering Options:** Offer catering services for parties, corporate events, and special occasions.

- **Customization:** Allow customers to customize their pizzas with a variety of toppings and crust options.

Before introducing new items, thoroughly test them and gather feedback from your staff and trusted customers.

9.2 Catering & Special Events: Serving Pizza beyond Your Pizzeria

Catering and special events can be a lucrative source of revenue for your pizzeria. It allows you to reach a wider audience and showcase your culinary skills. Consider these opportunities:

- **Corporate Events:** Cater lunches, meetings, or company parties.
- **Private Parties:** Cater birthday parties, family gatherings, or other special occasions.
- **Weddings:** Offer customized pizza stations or full-service catering for weddings.
- **Festivals and Fairs:** Set up a pizza booth at local festivals or fairs.
- **School Events:** Cater school events like sports games or fundraisers.

Invest in proper catering equipment, such as portable ovens, chafing dishes, and serving platters. Promote your catering services on your website, social media, and through local partnerships.

9.3 Franchising Your Pizzeria: Taking Your Brand to New Locations

If your pizzeria is successful, franchising could be a viable option for expanding your brand and increasing revenue. Franchising involves licensing your business model, brand, and recipes to other entrepreneurs who open their own pizzerias under your name.

Franchising requires careful planning and execution. You'll need to develop a comprehensive franchise agreement, provide training and support to your franchisees, and maintain quality control across all locations. While franchising can be a profitable way to grow your business, it also comes with risks and challenges. Consider seeking professional advice before embarking on this path.

9.4 Offering Delivery & Takeout: Expanding Your Pizzeria's Reach

Delivery and takeout can significantly expand your customer base and increase sales. It allows you to reach customers who may not be able to visit your pizzeria in person.

- **In-House Delivery:** Hire delivery drivers or partner with a third-party delivery service.
- **Online Ordering:** Set up an online ordering system to streamline the process for customers.
- **Takeout Specials:** Offer discounts or promotions for takeout orders to incentivize customers.

- **Packaging:** Invest in high-quality packaging that keeps your pizzas hot and fresh during transit.

By offering delivery and takeout, you can cater to the growing demand for convenience and reach a wider audience.

9.5 Exploring Partnerships: Collaborating with Local Businesses

Partnering with other local businesses can be a mutually beneficial way to promote your pizzeria and expand your reach. Consider these possibilities:

- **Cross-Promotion:** Offer discounts to customers of partner businesses, or vice versa.
- **Joint Events:** Host joint events or promotions with other businesses.
- **Product Collaborations:** Create unique menu items or specials featuring products from partner businesses.
- **Community Sponsorships:** Sponsor local sports teams, charities, or events to increase brand visibility.

By collaborating with other businesses, you can tap into their customer base and strengthen your presence in the community.

9.6 Investing in Technology: Enhancing Efficiency & Customer Experience

Technology can be a powerful tool for improving your pizzeria's efficiency, customer experience, and bottom line. Consider these technology solutions:

- **POS Systems:** Streamline ordering, payment processing, and inventory management.
- **Online Ordering:** Allow customers to order online for pickup or delivery.
- **Delivery Apps:** Partner with delivery apps to reach a wider audience.
- **Tabletop Ordering Tablets:** Enable customers to order and pay at their table.
- **Kitchen Display Systems (KDS):** Improve communication between the kitchen and front-of-house staff.
- **Customer Relationship Management (CRM) Software:** Track customer data, personalize marketing messages, and build loyalty.
- **Social Media Management Tools:** Schedule posts, track engagement, and analyze social media performance.

By embracing technology, you can streamline operations, reduce costs, improve customer service, and gain a competitive edge.

9.7 Staying Ahead of the Competition: Adapting to Market Trends

The pizza industry is constantly evolving. To stay ahead of the competition, it's crucial to stay informed about the latest trends and adapt your business accordingly.

- **Emerging Food Trends:** Keep an eye on emerging food trends, such as plant-based pizzas, gluten-free options, or unique flavor combinations.
- **Technological Advancements:** Embrace new technologies that can improve efficiency and customer experience, such as online ordering, delivery apps, and self-service kiosks.
- **Customer Preferences:** Pay attention to customer feedback and adjust your menu, service, and atmosphere to meet their evolving needs and preferences.
- **Competitor Analysis:** Monitor your competitors to see what they're doing well and where they're falling short. Use this information to identify areas where you can differentiate yourself.
- **Innovation:** Don't be afraid to experiment with new ideas and concepts. Innovation can help you attract new customers and keep your existing ones engaged.

By staying ahead of the curve and adapting to market trends, you can ensure that your pizzeria remains relevant and continues to grow.

Growth is essential for the long-term success of your pizzeria. By expanding your menu, offering catering and special events, considering franchising, expanding your reach with delivery and takeout, exploring partnerships, investing in technology, and staying ahead of the competition, you can take your pizzeria to new heights. Remember, growth requires a strategic approach, adaptability, and a willingness to embrace new ideas. With the right mindset and strategies, you can build a pizzeria that thrives for years to come.

Chapter 10

The Future of Your Pizzeria

In the final chapter of this guide, we'll shift our focus from the day-to-day operations of your pizzeria to the long-term vision for your business. This includes evaluating your current success, setting new goals, embracing innovation, and considering the legacy you want to leave behind. We'll also explore options for exiting your business, giving back to the community, and reflecting on your journey as a pizzapreneur.

10.1 Evaluating Your Pizzeria's Success: Measuring Key Performance Indicators

To gauge your pizzeria's success and identify areas for improvement, it's essential to track key performance indicators (KPIs). These are quantifiable metrics that reflect your business's performance in various areas. Some essential KPIs for pizzerias include:

- **Sales Revenue:** Track your total sales revenue over time, as well as sales by category (dine-in, takeout, delivery) and by menu item. This will help you identify your most popular items and areas for growth.
- **Profit Margin:** Calculate your gross profit margin (revenue minus cost of goods sold) and net profit margin (revenue minus all expenses). This will give you a clear picture of your pizzeria's profitability.

- **Customer Satisfaction:** Gather feedback from customers through surveys, online reviews, and social media. Track customer satisfaction ratings to gauge how well you're meeting their expectations.
- **Employee Satisfaction:** Conduct employee surveys or interviews to measure job satisfaction and identify areas for improvement in your workplace culture.
- **Table Turnover Rate:** Track how quickly tables are turned over during peak hours. This can help you optimize seating capacity and maximize revenue.
- **Food Cost Percentage:** Calculate the percentage of your revenue that goes towards food costs. This will help you identify areas where you can reduce waste and improve efficiency.
- **Labor Cost Percentage:** Calculate the percentage of your revenue that goes towards labor costs. This will help you manage staffing levels and optimize labor efficiency.

By regularly tracking and analyzing these KPIs, you can gain valuable insights into your pizzeria's performance, identify areas for improvement, and make data-driven decisions to drive growth.

10.2 Setting New Goals for Growth: Expanding Your Pizzeria's Reach

Once you've evaluated your pizzeria's current success, it's time to set new goals for growth. This could involve:

- **Opening New Locations:** If your pizzeria is thriving, consider expanding to new locations. Conduct thorough market research to identify potential areas for expansion and ensure your brand can successfully translate to new markets.
- **Expanding Your Menu:** Introduce new pizza flavors, seasonal specials, or non-pizza items to attract new customers and keep existing ones engaged.
- **Offering Delivery and Takeout:** Reach a wider audience by offering delivery and takeout options.
- **Catering to Special Events:** Expand your business by catering to corporate events, weddings, parties, and other special occasions.
- **Increasing Marketing Efforts:** Invest in marketing campaigns to raise brand awareness, attract new customers, and drive traffic to your pizzeria.
- **Improving Operational Efficiency:** Implement systems and processes to streamline operations, reduce costs, and improve profitability.

Remember, growth requires careful planning and execution. Set realistic goals, allocate resources wisely, and monitor your progress closely to ensure you're on track.

10.3 Embracing Innovation: New Pizza Trends & Technology

The pizza industry is constantly evolving, with new trends and technologies emerging all the time. To stay competitive, it's important to embrace innovation and stay ahead of the curve. This could involve:

- **New Pizza Styles:** Experiment with emerging pizza styles, such as Detroit-style, Grandma-style, or artisanal pizzas with unique crusts and toppings.
- **Healthier Options:** Cater to health-conscious consumers by offering gluten-free, vegan, or low-calorie pizza options.
- **Technology Integration:** Embrace new technologies like online ordering, delivery apps, tabletop ordering tablets, and AI-powered chatbots to enhance the customer experience and streamline operations.
- **Sustainable Practices:** Implement sustainable practices, such as using compostable packaging, sourcing local ingredients, or reducing food waste.

By embracing innovation, you can differentiate your pizzeria from the competition, attract new customers, and keep your brand fresh and relevant.

10.4 Building a Pizzeria Legacy: Passing on Your Pizza Passion

If you've built a successful pizzeria, you may want to consider how to pass on your legacy to future generations. This could involve:

- **Family Succession:** If you have children or other family members who are interested in the business, you can groom them to take over the reins.
- **Selling Your Business:** If you're ready to retire or move on to other ventures, you can sell your pizzeria to another entrepreneur.

- **Franchising:** If your brand is strong and your business model is replicable, you can franchise your pizzeria to expand to new locations.
- **Creating a Scholarship or Foundation:** You can create a scholarship or foundation to support aspiring pizza makers or entrepreneurs.
- **Writing a Cookbook or Memoir:** Share your recipes, stories, and insights with others through a cookbook or memoir.

By building a legacy, you ensure that your pizza passion lives on and continues to inspire others.

10.5 Selling Your Pizzeria: Exiting Your Business Strategically

If you decide to sell your pizzeria, it's important to approach the process strategically. Here are some key considerations:

- **Timing:** Choose the right time to sell based on market conditions, your personal goals, and your pizzeria's financial performance.
- **Valuation:** Get a professional valuation of your business to determine its fair market value.
- **Marketing:** Market your pizzeria to potential buyers through business brokers, online listings, or word-of-mouth.
- **Negotiation:** Negotiate the terms of the sale, including the purchase price, payment terms, and any contingencies.
- **Transition:** Plan for a smooth transition by training the new owner and providing support during the handover process.

By planning your exit strategically, you can maximize your return on investment and ensure a smooth transition for your staff and customers.

10.6 Giving Back to the Community: Supporting Local Causes

As a local business owner, you have the opportunity to make a positive impact on your community. Consider giving back by:

- **Donating to Charities:** Donate a portion of your profits to local charities or organizations.
- **Sponsoring Events:** Sponsor local sports teams, school events, or community festivals.
- **Hosting Fundraisers:** Host fundraising events for local causes.
- **Offering Discounts:** Offer discounts to first responders, teachers, or other community members.
- **Volunteering Your Time:** Volunteer your time or resources to local organizations or initiatives.

By giving back to your community, you build goodwill, strengthen your brand, and create a positive impact on the world around you.

10.7 The Pizzapreneur's Journey: Reflecting on Your Pizzeria Success

As you reflect on your journey as a pizzapreneur, take time to celebrate your achievements and learn from your challenges. Consider these questions:

- What are you most proud of?
- What have you learned along the way?
- What advice would you give to aspiring pizzapreneurs?
- What are your plans for the future?

Remember, the journey is just as important as the destination. Embrace the challenges, celebrate the successes, and never stop learning and growing as a pizzapreneur.

www.ingramcontent.com/pod-product-compliance
Lightning Source LLC
Chambersburg PA
CBHW050235230526
45470CB00005B/1959